Table of Contents

D1568851

Introduction

A Word from the Author i

Showcase

A Color Gallery of Carvings 1

Research

Researching Big Cats 5

Technique

Techniques for Big Cats...15

Step-by-Step

Carving, Burning and Painting a Lion 27

Patterns

Using, Altering and Creating Patterns...................44

    Lion Pattern 45

    Lioness Pattern..46

    Jaguar Pattern...47

    Tiger Pattern 48

    Cub Pattern...49

    Lioness with Cub 50

Index

Index 51

Introduction

Several years ago, I was approached to do a book on sculpting mammals from wood. The first thing I did was set objectives that I thought were appropriate for my style and, more importantly, for those interested in the book. When I was asked to continue the series with a book on lions, tigers and jaguars, it was important to me to make additions that would enhance the quality and continue what was set forth in the first book. One of the great improvements was something with which I had nothing to do—producing the book in color. I think this will greatly enhance certain points in each chapter, ranging from the carving projects themselves to color-coded drawings.

The new charts and the drawings have been improved as well. There are skeleton sketches showing color-coded points of reference to compare the skeletons of the different species. Using these joints, or pivot points, you can redesign the projects presented here to your own liking. The drawings have been shaded in areas that will be recessed on the patterns. I tried to utilize resources such as museums and conservation centers to research live and dead animals. I've also expanded these reference sections to include things such as feet.

I have also included information on the animals to increase your knowledge of them, as well as to foster an awareness of each animal's personality. You can further your knowledge by reading up on lions, tigers and jaguars or even do some deeper digging into other species. This is an important part of carving, and one that is often overlooked.

The poses in the pattern section were designed to be interchangeable. For example, the pose of the jaguar can be adapted to that of the tiger. After studying the reference material and making a few adjustments to the proportions, you can even come up with several different patterns on your own!

As the title implies, this is an "artistic approach" to carving. I have included a step-by-step demonstration on carving, burning and painting a lion, but I wish to emphasize that I feel this type of presentation limits the abilities of any carver. My main intention for including a demonstration in this book is for the reader to use it as a guide. It is meant to show you the flexibility in adapting certain ideas that you may find relevant and combining them with your own unique style. As you progress through the book, keep in mind that experimenting and changing your projects to suit your needs will only enhance your final result.—*Desiree Hajny*

Photography credits: Top right: Noble Curiosity (Cheetah), *by Desiree Hajny, 1990. Center left:* Regal Thirst (Cheetah), *by Desiree Hajny, 1989. Bottom right:* Himalayan Scratching Post (Snow Leopards), *by Desiree Hajny, 1995. Photos by Mike Hutmacher.*

Jaguar, *by Desiree Hajny, pattern on page 47.*

Elegance (*Black Panther*), *by Desiree Hajny, 1995.*

Big Cats

1

Lion, *by Desiree Hajny, pattern on page 45.*

Lioness, *by Desiree Hajny,*
pattern on page 46.

Tiger, *by Desiree Hajny, pattern on page 48.*

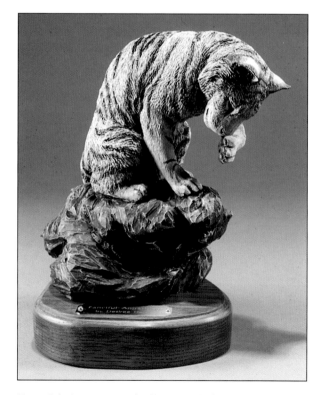

Fanciful Apparition *(White Tiger), by Desiree Hajny,* 1995.

Researching Big Cats

Research is an important part of any carving project—and one that is often overlooked. It is important to remember that the more you know about your subject, the more realistic your final piece will be.

Research can be conducted in any number of ways. Encyclopedias and other reference books featuring animals are good places to start. Magazines, calendars and other publications with full-color photographs are also good sources of reference material. Live animals can be studied at zoos or with the aid of video tapes. Many universities and museums have taxidermy mounts or study skins for reference.

Lions, unlike other cats, live in groups called prides. A pride may have anywhere from 4-30 members.

The information presented in this chapter was gleaned from a number of sources. You'll find reference photos, anatomy drawings and reference sketches. Use this information as a starting point and then conduct more research to gain additional information specific to your particular project.

Tip: The more you know about your subject the more realistic your final piece will be. You can never have too much reference material.

Tigers

Tigers are admired by many for the combination of beauty and strength they possess. Many also fear tigers, but in fact, most tigers will run away from people unless they are faced with a desperate situation.

Tigers once roamed over much of Asia, the frozen North, the mountains of Central Asia and the steamy jungles of the South. Although tigers can live in many different locales, they have not been able to live alongside of man. For the past 200 years, the number of tigers in the wild have dwindled. There are an estimated 5,000 tigers left in the wild.

Lions are great hunters. Their eyes, larger than the eyes of any other meat-eating animal, are specially designed for night vision. Large, sensitive ears allow them to detect prey up to a mile away.

Tigers are known to live for about 20 years if they are left undisturbed. The females tend to live longer lives, mainly due to the fact that the males live more dangerous lives battling other males.

It is difficult to tell male and female tigers apart, unless the female is with cubs. There is a significant difference in size, however. The adult male can weigh about 420 pounds; the female about 100 pounds less. The male averages about seven feet from head to rear, and the female is about a foot shorter. The largest tiger ever measured was a Siberian tiger that weighed over 700 pounds and measured nine feet in length.

At birth, young tigers will average about 12 inches in length and weigh less than two pounds. Two, three or four cubs are present at birth. They will stay with their mother for three to four years. Cubs are usually ready for their first hunt at about six months and, in a year's time, will be able to hunt deer or buffalo.

There are six known species of tigers. The Caspian tiger is now extinct. The Bengal tiger is the most common. There are about 2,500 Bengals left, with most located in India. The Siberian tiger is the largest and lives in the coldest climate. There are about 200 Siberian tigers left. There are known to be about 100 Chinese tigers living. The Sumatran and Javan tigers live on

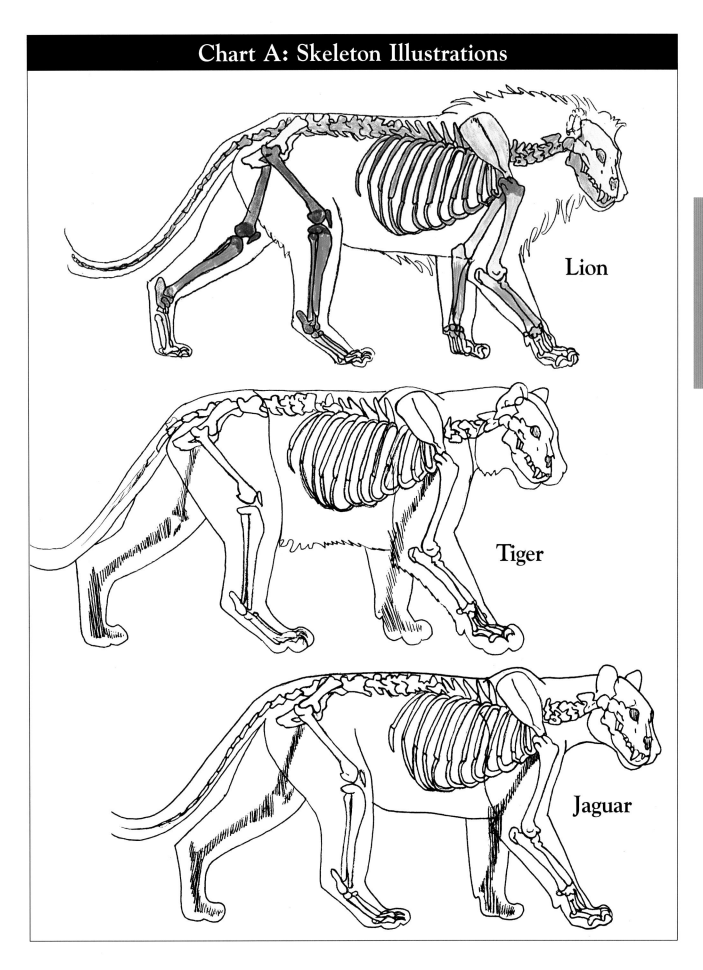

Lion

Research

Tiger

Jaguar

Choosing an expression for your cat is an important part of planning your carving. This young male lion, photographed in Kenya, snarls a warning in the photographer's direction. Note how the skin above the nose wrinkles.

islands south of the Asian continent. They are smaller than other tigers, which allows them easier movement through their jungle habitat. There are about 30 of these cats in existence.

Tigers may be more adept at capturing large prey than any other animal. They have longer canine teeth than any other predator, and the muscle development of tigers allows them to jump ten yards on level ground and 15 feet into the air. Tigers are also good swimmers.

In one year, a tiger can eat 70 large animals. It will hunt water buffalo, deer, wild pigs and other large animals. A tiger will take on a much larger animal if it is unable to find something available and suitable for consumption. Tigers are solitary hunters. Lack of excessive prey prevents them from hunting in groups. For every animal a tiger snares for food, about twenty escape. A tiger needs about 15 pounds of food each day to survive.

If tigers didn't have stripes, they probably wouldn't survive in the wild. Tigers are not fast runners, and the markings provide them with excellent camouflage. No two tigers have exactly the same markings, much like no two

Chart B: Skull

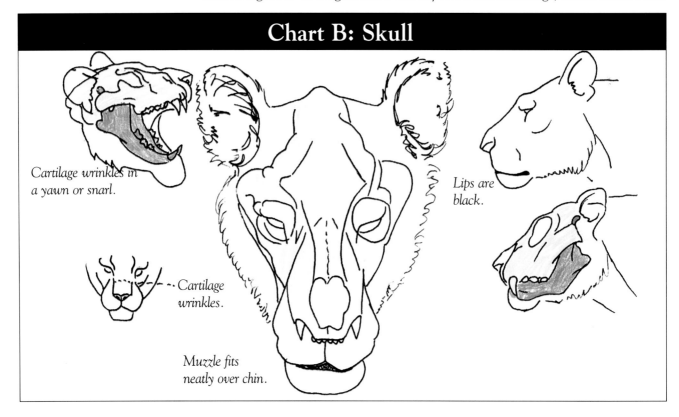

Cartilage wrinkles in a yawn or snarl.

Cartilage wrinkles.

Muzzle fits neatly over chin.

Lips are black.

humans have the same fingerprints.

Every tiger has a private hunting area marked with a scent or with scratch marks made on a tree. When a tiger stalks prey, it usually hides first behind a tree, bush or rock. It attacks from behind. It will either bite the animal on the back of the neck or the throat to kill it. The tiger then drags its prey into the brush and buries what it doesn't eat for another time. Usually, a male tiger will share its kill with cubs, even if they aren't his cubs.

Research

Siberian Tigers

Siberian tigers are the largest living cats in the world. Found in the Amur-Ussuri region of Siberia and in Northern China and Korea, they possess both grace and beauty. The males measure 9–12 feet from head to tip of tail. The females are smaller. The males are about three-and-one-half feet tall at the shoulder and, on the average, weigh between 400–650 pounds.

The mane of a young male lion will become thicker as he grows older.

Siberian tigers become sexually mature three to five years after birth. There is no particular season for mating. The gestation period of the female is three to three-and-one-half months. The litter may have up to six cubs, but usually numbers three or four.

The male is a solitary animal. He will allow tigers of either sex to pass through his area, but is more tolerant of female tigers.

Siberian tigers have very large territories. Ranges of more than 4,000 square miles have been noted. One cat will occupy an area this large for

Tip: *Reference includes more than just photos of an animal. Look for taxidermy mounts, study skins, skeleton illustrations and muscle sketches.*

many years as long as the food source is adequate. If food becomes scarce, the tiger may migrate hundreds of miles.

Both males and females mark their territories with urine and by scratching trees. Only the male defends his territory against other males, perhaps to protect an area close to a female or a locale that is a valuable food source.

Because Siberian tigers have to withstand temperatures that may be as low as −50°F, they grow longer and thicker coats than other tigers. They also develop a layer of fat on their flanks and belly that helps to insulate their bodies.

The same lion pictured on the previous page here shows a more relaxed pose. Note how the ears lay back and his eyes close as he stretches.

A photograph of a charging jaguar provides a good look at the teeth and the inside of the cat's mouth. Note how the skin stretches around the mouth and nose while the mouth is open.

Siberian tigers are currently an endangered subspecies. There are probably about 200 of these animals left in the wild and about the same number in captivity.

Jaguars

Jaguars are powerful, stocky cats. Their size and spotted coats make them look similar to a heavy-set leopard. There are minor differences between the spot patterns of jaguars and leopards. The jaguars' fur varies from pale gold to rusty red and has a pattern of dark rosettes that enclose one or two smaller spots. The rosettes on a leopard's back do not have smaller spots inside them. There are also all-black jaguars, and sometimes the spots show through the darker background of the fur.

The stocky build of jaguars makes them look larger than they really are. The largest jaguars come from the Pantanal area of Brazil where males have weighed up to 300 pounds. In other areas, jaguars weigh much less. Males normally weigh about 120 pounds; females weigh about 80 pounds. The head and body length measures between 45 and 70 inches, and the tail length is between 18 and 30 inches, depending on region and sex.

Chart C: Leg Bones and Muscles

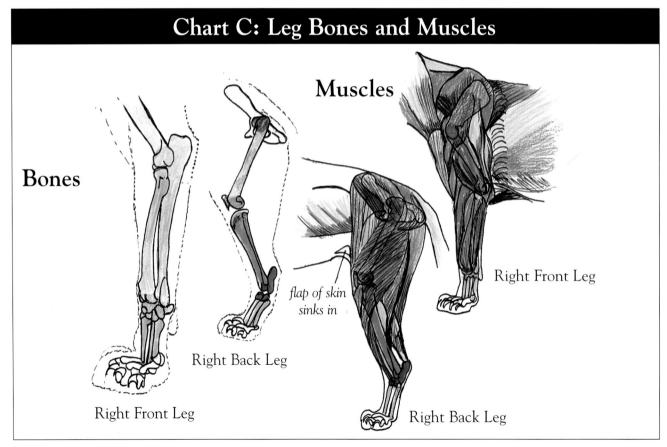

Bones

Muscles

Right Back Leg

flap of skin sinks in

Right Front Leg

Right Front Leg

Right Back Leg

Jaguars are found in well-watered areas, such as swampy grasslands and forests alongside streams, rivers and lakes. In the last 100 years, the jaguars' range has been greatly reduced. Their current range includes south-central Mexico, Central America and as far as northern Argentina in South America. Jaguars have also been spotted in Texas.

A jaguar's fur varies from pale gold to rusty red. The dark rosettes on its coat encircle one or two smaller spots.

The mother's gestation period ranges from three to three-and-one-half months. The young are about 30 ounces at birth and will remain with the mother for about two years. Usually, there are one to four cubs present at birth.

Jaguars are solitary animals. Their territories are determined by habitat, prey density and human disturbance in the area. Females have smaller ranges, as small as four square miles and as large as sixty-five miles. Males have larger ranges, usually from ten to sixty miles.

Jaguars will eat almost anything that is available. This includes snakes,

turtles, fish, small mammals, deer and cattle. The jaguar's powerful jaws and canine teeth allow it to kill livestock weighing three to four times its own weight. The cat often attacks with a bite to the back of the skull, rather than

Close study of a jaguar's facial markings shows how the sizes of the spots vary across the face.

Jaguars prefer areas with a plentiful water source. This jaguar was photographed in the rainforests of Belize.

the bite to the throat or neck that is often used by other large cats. Jaguars don't mind swimming. They will follow their prey into a stream. Or they might lie on a branch over the water and suddenly slap the water to grab a fish.

Experts estimate that there are about 10,000 jaguars in existence.

Lions

The strength and beauty of lions have fascinated people for many years. When you see a male lion with its magnificent mane and proud walk, it's easy to understand why the lion has been called the "king of the beasts."

Lions are included in the big cat family. The most significant difference between big cats and other cats is that the big cats can roar, but not purr. Other cats can purr, but not roar.

Chart D: Bone Movement While Walking

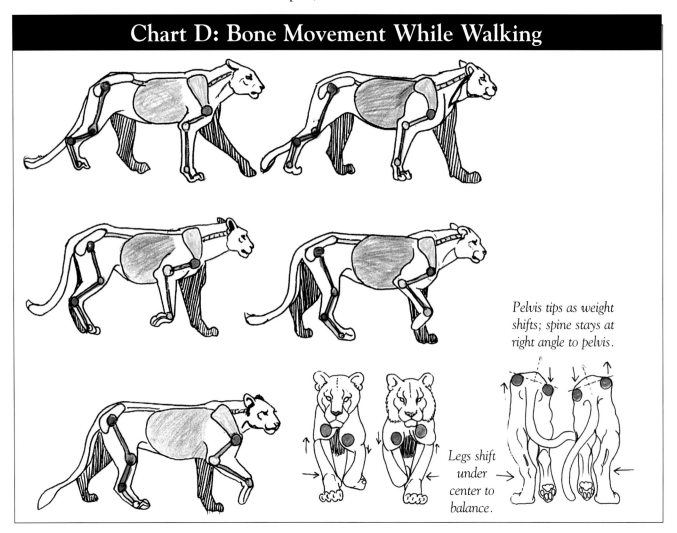

Pelvis tips as weight shifts; spine stays at right angle to pelvis.

Legs shift under center to balance.

Only Siberian tigers are larger than lions. Male lions may be nine to ten feet in length and weigh around 500 pounds. Females are about seven to eight feet in length and weigh from 270 to 350 pounds.

Lions are different from other cats in that they live in groups. These groups, or prides, have anywhere from 4 to 30 members. This pride includes several females and their young and one or more males. The females in a pride usually stay together for life, but the males come and go. Oftentimes they are challenged by other males, with the winner staying and the defeated male going on to live by himself or join a group of other males.

Cubs make interesting subjects to carve. This lion cub sports large paws that seem to be too big for his growing body.

Lions also hunt together. Living in groups allows lions to be more successful in hunting and seizing food. A lion that hunts alone may have a hard time catching its prey.

Much of the hunting is done by a team of females. The lion team usually divides into two groups. One group circles around to get ahead of the prey. The other group then shows itself and scares the prey. The frightened animals stampede into the first group of lions.

The lions' coloring allows them to blend in when approaching and attacking their prey. Lions will try to get very close to their prey before attacking it by making a big leap and grabbing it. Lions have strong muscles in their legs. These muscles allow them to leap through the air up to 35 feet in a single jump. The lions' eyes are the biggest of any meat-eating animal, and their ears allow them to hear prey that is as far away as a mile. Their eyes are made specifically for seeing at night.

Tip: *Collect reference on your subject's habitat, too. Mammals are often colored to blend into their habitat and that coloring may vary with their surroundings and the time of year.*

Larger animals are the lions' preferred prey, because they provide more meat. Lions are good hunters, but they miss more prey than they catch. Lions may go for days without eating. Lions sometimes get their food by taking it from other animals, as this is often much easier than hunting. If lions can't find enough of their regular prey, they will eat smaller animals such as hares, tortoises and even porcupines. If food is really scarce, lions will resort to eating anything they can find, from snakes to rotten wood.

At birth, lion cubs are blind and helpless. They weigh less than five pounds. Usually there are three cubs in a litter, but sometimes there may be

Lion cubs are born blind and helpless. They will spend the first few weeks of life with their mother hidden away from the rest of the pride.

A male lion can weigh up to 500 pounds. Females are slightly smaller and weigh from 270-350 pounds.

as many as five. The first few weeks of the cubs' lives are spent hidden from the pride. The mother then brings them out to join the rest of the family.

In a pride, all the mothers take care of the cubs. When the adults are off on a hunt, the mother hides the cubs among the rocks or high grass. The males are also very patient with the cubs.

Most of the lions in the world are either African or Asiatic lions. The African lions live on the grassy plains of Africa. The few Asiatic lions that remain live on a small wildlife preserve in India. At one time there were lions on every continent except Antarctica and Australia.

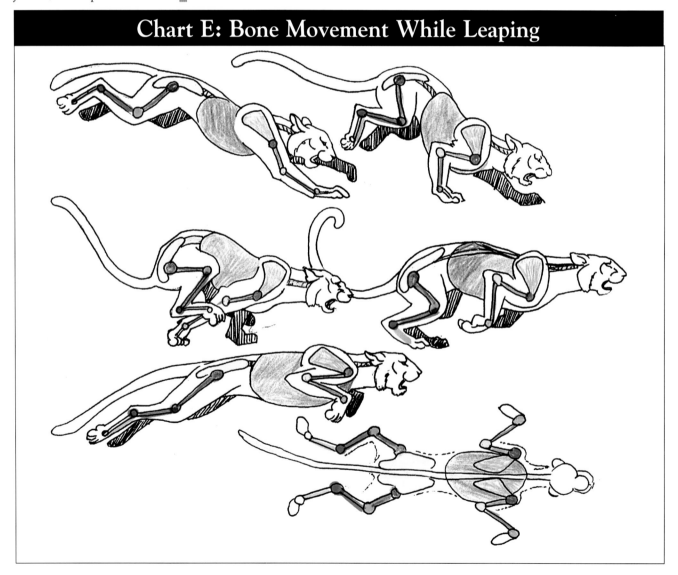

Chart E: Bone Movement While Leaping

Techniques for Big Cats

The projects in this book are all carved from basswood. This is the wood that I feel most comfortable using. Please feel free to exercise that same option and use the type of wood with which you feel most comfortable. The dimensions listed in the pattern section are my suggestions for these cats. However, feel free to reduce or enlarge the sizes to adapt them to meet your needs. I have

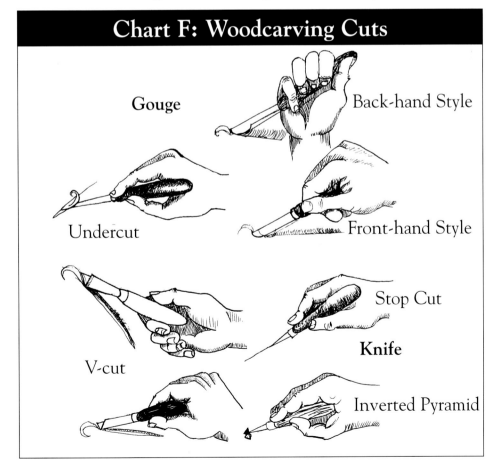

Chart F: Woodcarving Cuts

Gouge

Back-hand Style

Undercut

Front-hand Style

V-cut

Stop Cut

Knife

Inverted Pyramid

Tip: *For safety's sake, remember to keep your tools sharp and to always cut away from yourself. A protective glove will help to safeguard the hand that is holding the carving.*

Warning

Angry

Content

Cats display a variety of emotions. Take their expressions into consideration when you are planning your carving.

provided plenty of information—from bone structure charts to muscle illustrations—to do some redesigning, such as turning the head or altering the animal's pose. Use these charts to mold the patterns in this book to your own ideas.

For all of the patterns, with the exception of the lion, the grain should run vertically. With the pose of the lion, you could have the grain run horizontally or vertically. Make sure the grain runs in the correct direction; this will add strength to the legs. It took me several years of carving and much gluing and repairing before I learned this lesson.

Once you've decided which of the cats you are going to carve, draw a side-view pattern on the wood using carbon paper. You can also trace around a cut-out pattern with a pencil or knife or trace the pattern onto acetate.

If you are using carbon paper to transfer your pattern to the block of wood, simply place a piece of carbon paper, carbon side down, on the block. Place your pattern on top of the carbon paper. Using a pointed object like a pen or pencil, trace along the lines of the pattern. When you remove the pattern and carbon paper, the outline will appear on the wood. Following the lines, cut the wood on a bandsaw. Repeat this process on the sides and top of

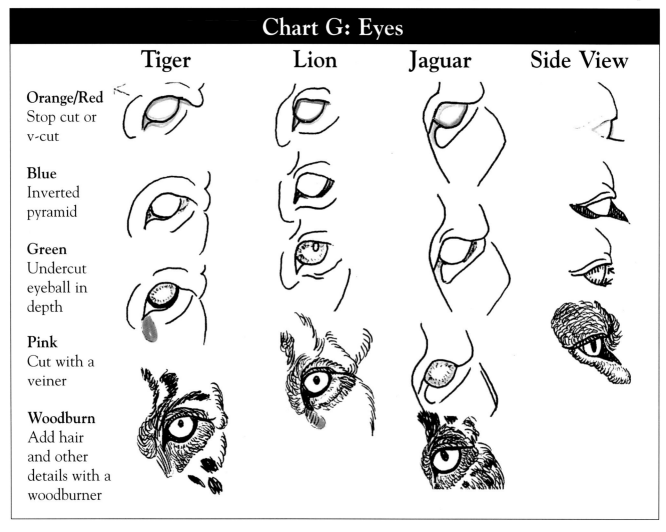

Chart G: Eyes

	Tiger	Lion	Jaguar	Side View
Orange/Red Stop cut or v-cut				
Blue Inverted pyramid				
Green Undercut eyeball in depth				
Pink Cut with a veiner				
Woodburn Add hair and other details with a woodburner				

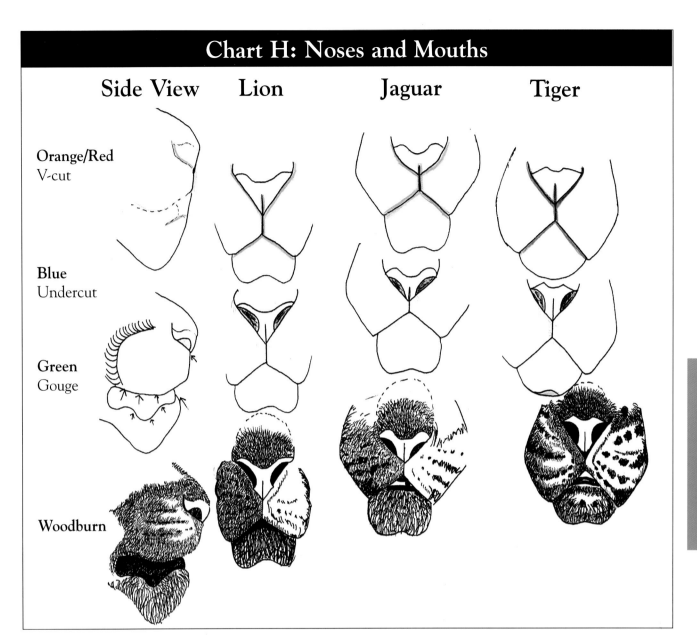

Chart H: Noses and Mouths

Side View	Lion	Jaguar	Tiger

Orange/Red
V-cut

Blue
Undercut

Green
Gouge

Woodburn

the block.

Once the wood has been cut to the pattern shape, use the top view of the pattern to sketch in the top parts of the body on the cut-out. On both sides of the cut-out, carve to those lines. At this time, leave the base area alone. If you've altered the design, leave some extra wood to accommodate for the changes in the body shape. Remove enough wood to show the curves and contours pictured in the drawings and on your pattern.

Whenever I do a carving, my first challenge is roughing in the subject's head. I find that if I can get the face carved to my liking, a personality will emerge. Plus, it takes some of the pressure off. I figure if the head doesn't turn out the way I want it to, it's easier for me to scrap the entire project at this

Use a pencil to check the proportions of the face.

point and start over. Study Chart B: Skull (page 8) for an inside view of the head and the location of the jaw pivot, eye, nose and ear. Now, from the top view, draw in the facial features using Chart G: Eyes (page 16) and Chart H: Noses and Mouths (page 17). The centerline of the head is vital. Pay close attention to it on the pattern and the charts. Mark in the bridge of the nose and the eye socket area. Paying close attention to the bridge of the nose and using the front and side view patterns, use a #6 gouge, 1/4", (rotary, use Kutzall Burr gouge cut, ball-shaped, 1/4" x 1/2" x 1/2") on both sides, tapering the nose down and behind the muzzle. Leave the top of the bridge of the nose flat. It is important to remember that you are tapering on each side. Cats have binoc-

Chart I: Ears

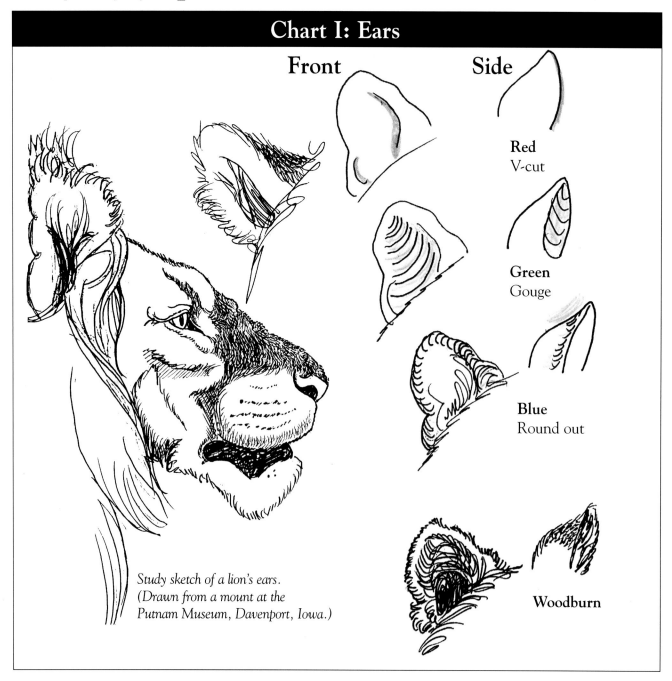

Front   Side

Red
V-cut

Green
Gouge

Blue
Round out

Woodburn

*Study sketch of a lion's ears.
(Drawn from a mount at the
Putnam Museum, Davenport, Iowa.)*

ular vision which allows them to focus and converge on prey. Refer to Chart B: Skull (page 8) to set the sockets. Gouge out the areas where the eye sockets are, keeping in mind that the eyes are positioned forward.

The age of the cat can influence the look of the eyes. An older cat may have sagging lids and bags under its eyes. The bilateral symmetry of the eye placement of the older cat may not be as perfect as that of a younger feline. If you are carving a younger cat, the bilateral symmetry will allow for the eyeball placement to be right-angled to the center point. The eyeballs can be set anywhere in the socket. The eye sockets are always at a right angle to the centerline. (See Chart B: Skull, page 8.)

The area under the cheekbones of your cat will sink in. As you make these cuts, use gentle swoops with a #5 or #6 gouge (rotary, Kutzall Carbide Burr gouge cut, ball-shaped, $1/4$" x $1/2$"x $1/2$"). Refer to your pattern for an accurate depth of the sweeps.

On the temple area, again use a #5 or #6 gouge (rotary, Carbide Kutzall Burr gouge cut, ball-shaped, $1/4$" x $1/2$" x $1/2$") for the area between the eyes and ears. Sink your tool into the wood gently. The depth of the cut will be different, depending on the species you are carving.

When starting on the face, there are many slight differences to consider. Don't forget the mood of your chosen subject. For example, if the cat you are carving is angry, some areas on the nose will wrinkle, and the muzzle will pull up to reveal the top cuspids. For whichever cat you are carving, refer to Chart G: Eyes (page 16), Chart H: Noses and Mouths (page 17) and Chart I: Ears (page 18).

Tip: When transferring your pattern to a block of wood, be sure the grain runs in the correct direction. Small, delicate parts, like tails and legs, may break otherwise.

Technique

When you are ready to begin the body, look at your pattern again and begin by drawing in the spine. This serves as a centerline. The backbone, shown in pink on Chart A: Skeleton Illustrations (page 7), serves as the centerline. Taper the shoulder blade area using gouge #4 or #5, $1/2$", (rotary, Carbide Kutzall Burr heavy shaping, cone-shaped, $1/4$" x $3/4$" x $3/8$"). The shoulder blades are not fused to the backbone. The blades are connected by tendons and ligaments. Imagine these as rubber bands providing that extra stretch needed in particular positions. Take a look at Chart C: Leg Bones and Muscles (page 10) for an in-depth study on muscle structure of the shoulder blade area and the front legs. Keep in mind that as the animal moves, some of these muscles bulge or stretch out. (These charts are color-coded to Chart A: Skeleton Illustrations, page 7, for easier understanding of the underlying structure.) Then taper the top part of the rib cage in toward the backbone using gouge #4 or #5, $1/2$" (rotary, Carbide Kutzall Burr, cone-shaped, $1/4$" x $3/4$" x $3/8$"). On the back end of the shoulder blade there is a recessed area. This space allows for movement when the animal is in motion. Refer to Chart D: Bone Movement While Walking (page 12) and Chart E: Bone Movement While Leaping (page 14) to see the movement. Use a #7 or #8, $1/2$", (rotary, Carbide Kutzall Burr, ball-shaped, $1/4$" x $1/2$" x $1/2$") to work this area.

The pelvis consists of six points that push the skin up. There are three

Black lips stretch in yawn or snarl on all three cats.

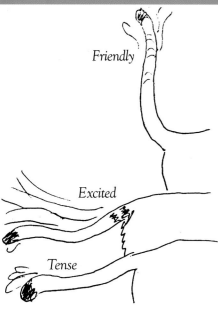

Friendly

Excited

Tense

A cat's tail shows emotion as well. Be sure to position the tail accordingly.

on each side of the spine. The pelvis is fused to the backbone. This makes the points at right angles to each other across the backbone, or centerline. When the cat is in motion, the pelvis is always at a right angle to the spine (or the centerline). Take a peek at Chart D: Bone Movement While Walking (page 12) to see for yourself.

The lumbar region, which refers to the spine between the end of the ribs and the pelvis, and pelvis itself function together as the animal moves. The lumbar region is marked in pink between the brown rib cage and the yellow pelvis on Chart A: Skeleton Illustrations (page 7). This area of the spine is very flexible to accommodate the movement of the pelvis area. It sinks in between the ribs and the legs from the side view to allow for back leg movement.

The legs hang down from the middle point of the pelvis on either side (on Chart C it is marked with brown). The belly tapers under the body and is rounded. If you are doing an older cat, keep in mind that there is more loose skin. The skin swings back and forth as the cat moves.

The legs that bear weight in movement angle under the body centerline.

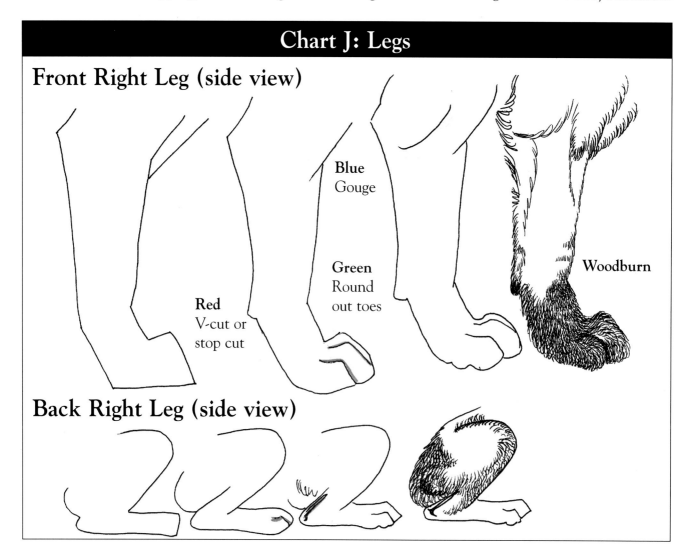

Chart J: Legs

Front Right Leg (side view)

Red
V-cut or stop cut

Blue
Gouge

Green
Round out toes

Woodburn

Back Right Leg (side view)

Chart K: Feet

Front View

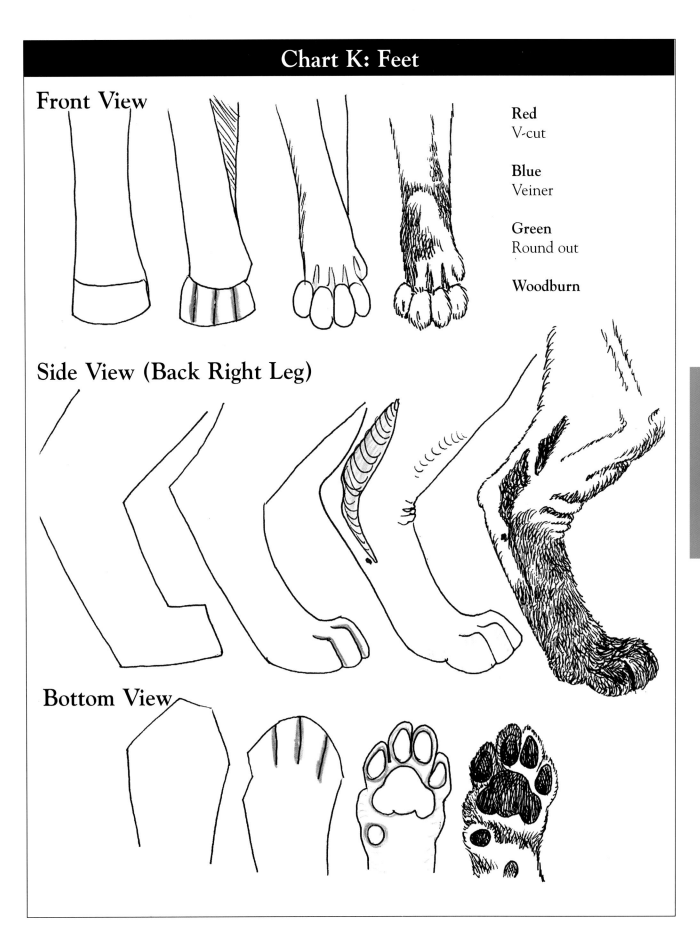

Red
V-cut

Blue
Veiner

Green
Round out

Woodburn

Side View (Back Right Leg)

Technique

Bottom View

Chart L: Common Woodburning Mistakes

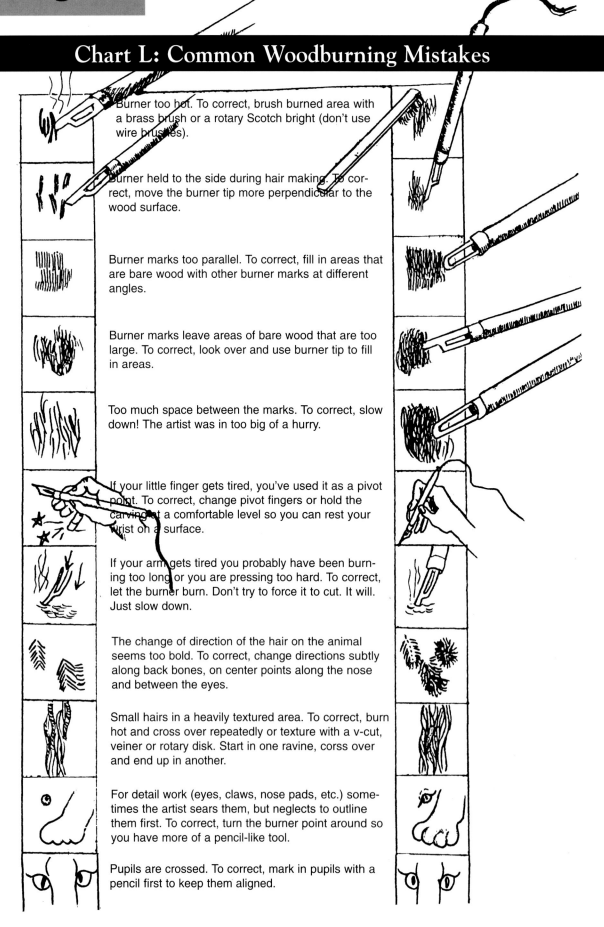

Burner too hot. To correct, brush burned area with a brass brush or a rotary Scotch bright (don't use wire brushes).

Burner held to the side during hair making. To correct, move the burner tip more perpendicular to the wood surface.

Burner marks too parallel. To correct, fill in areas that are bare wood with other burner marks at different angles.

Burner marks leave areas of bare wood that are too large. To correct, look over and use burner tip to fill in areas.

Too much space between the marks. To correct, slow down! The artist was in too big of a hurry.

If your little finger gets tired, you've used it as a pivot point. To correct, change pivot fingers or hold the carving at a comfortable level so you can rest your wrist on a surface.

If your arm gets tired you probably have been burning too long or you are pressing too hard. To correct, let the burner burn. Don't try to force it to cut. It will. Just slow down.

The change of direction of the hair on the animal seems too bold. To correct, change directions subtly along back bones, on center points along the nose and between the eyes.

Small hairs in a heavily textured area. To correct, burn hot and cross over repeatedly or texture with a v-cut, veiner or rotary disk. Start in one ravine, corss over and end up in another.

For detail work (eyes, claws, nose pads, etc.) sometimes the artist sears them, but neglects to outline them first. To correct, turn the burner point around so you have more of a pencil-like tool.

Pupils are crossed. To correct, mark in pupils with a pencil first to keep them aligned.

The leg that is bearing the most weight, front or back view, is pushed up. This includes the shoulder and the scapula. The shoulder is marked in purple and the scapula is marked in light blue on Chart A: Skeleton Illustrations (page 7). The pelvis tilts up in back (See Chart D: Bone Movement While Walking, page 12). On the jaguar pose, the legs angle out from the body and fit around the object the cat is lying on. Be aware that the bones form straight lines; the joints allow for bending. The high points on the pelvis stick out. While shaping the body, be aware of the rib cage—is it hanging or is it being pushed up as in the case of the Jaguar pose?

Shape up the feet by following Chart J: Legs (page 20) and Chart K: Feet (page 21). Study these charts as well for leg shaping. For redesigning legs, study leg movement on Chart D: Bone Movement While Walking (page 12) and Chart E: Bone Movement While Leaping (page 14). Chart C: Leg Bones and Muscles (page 10) shows a close-up of the leg bones and the muscles. Keep in mind that with each movement these muscles will either bulge or stretch out. Apply your research skills to study the structure of the species you have decided to carve.

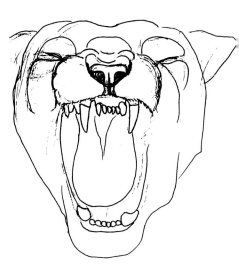

Texturing

Texturing your work effectively can enhance your piece greatly. When you are getting ready to texture, keep in mind that roughing up the wood doesn't have to be done. A desirable effect can be achieved through the use of a woodburner. If you're looking for a simpler message, you may not want to use texture at all. You can focus on the muscle groups to create a mood. Remember, if you are stylizing your piece, the use of shadows is important.

If you have decided to texture the piece, gouge the areas with the heaviest texture (rotary, various ball shapes). On a cat, these areas would be the belly, chest, neck, cheeks and side of the head. On a lion, the focus would be on the mane and the tip of the tail. Refer to Chart M: Tiger Hair Tract (page 24), Chart N: Lion Hair Tract (page 25) and Chart O: Jaguar Hair Tract (page 26). For a fierce or tense look, follow up the gouging with a parting tool (rotary, inverted cone or disk-shaped bit). If you are seeking a gentle look, use a softer veiner to break up the gouged area (rotary, rounded disk).

Follow the direction of the locks of hair using the hair tract charts as a guide for whichever cat you are carving. Note that the hair flow on the body of all three cats is similar. Those details are shown on Chart M: Tiger Hair Tract (page 24). The hair flow on the faces of the cats is slightly different and is shown on separate hair tract illustrations.

Woodburning

Any woodburner that has an adjustable thermostat will work well to show fur. There are many burner tips available on the market. Chart L: Burning (page 22) shows the ones that I normally use. You'll want to experiment with the tips you want to use, and again, use what you feel most comfortable with.

Tip: *When beginning to carve, take your subject's mood into consideration. The face muscles and skin will change position with each expression.*

Chart M: Tiger Hair Tract

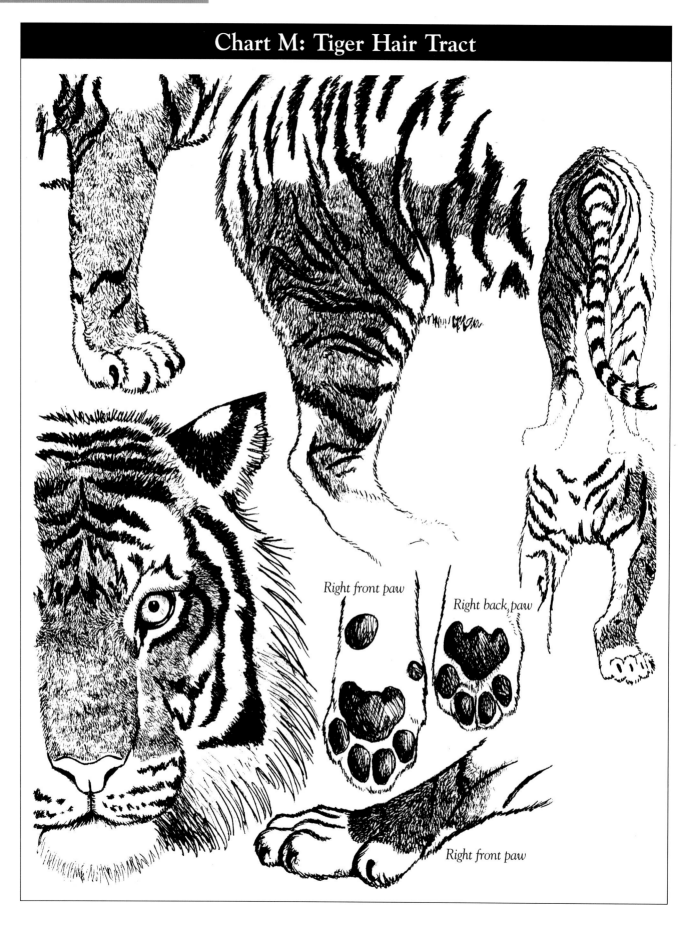

Right front paw

Right back paw

Right front paw

The hair tract drawings for each animal show how to begin burning the illusion of fur. Map out the direction of the fur first, considering gravity, the wind and the time of the year during which your animal is portrayed.

When you are ready to start with the actual burning, begin by making small marks with the burner tip you've chosen. Layer these marks and cross them over each other once in a while using a fluid motion. Animals don't have parallel hairs. The shortest hairs are on the face around the eyes and nose, so any tip that comes to a point will be helpful here.

Before you start on the eyes, mark the pupil in first with a pencil so you don't end up with a cross-eyed cat. Then, sear the wood of the eyeball with the side of a hot burning tip to get the shiny eyes. This will also seal the wood pores as it darkens it. The final finish will sit on top of the seared areas and give them a glistening effect. Use the point of your chosen burner tip to burn in the pupils. This depression in the eye area will make it easier to paint in the iris color. The claws on the cats will need to be seared also if the cat is in an aggressive pose. Big cats have retractable claws.

Painting

Whatever type of paint you choose, keep it thinned so the pigment doesn't clog up burn marks or carving details. There are many styles of painting and many different techniques. In fact, there are so many different styles to choose

Tip: *The hairs of your subject's fur do not lay parallel to each other. As you burn in the hairs, cross them over each other occasionally to create a more realistic effect.*

Tip: *Keep paints thinned. Thick paint will clog up burn marks and other texture.*

Chart N: Lion and Lioness Hair Tract

Painting

Study sketch of a jaguar snarl.

from that it is always comforting to know that there is no wrong or right way to paint. I like to allow the wood color to show through. This can be achieved by letting the colors bleed into one another by thinning down the pigment. It's up to you to choose what best fits your needs.

Before you begin, study the colors of your chosen animal. Be aware of the time of the year during which your cat is being portrayed; most animals are lighter in the wintertime to blend into the changing landscape. Start with light colors if you are using acrylics or water colors and gradually work in the dark colors. Start with dark colors if you are using oil paints and gradually work in the light colors. Be aware of the shadows throughout the carving and darken them. Use any excess paint on the habitat. Mammals generally are colored to blend into their habitat.

Dry brush areas with lighter colors. Use a stiff brush for this step and color the high points with just a hint of color. This sets off areas the sun would be hitting. Try dry brushing the habitat also.

Use a detail round brush to paint the colors of the eyes and other details of the face and body. Remember to lighten the upper part of the eyeball where the highlight is. After the paint dries, put a dull, clear finish over the entire piece.

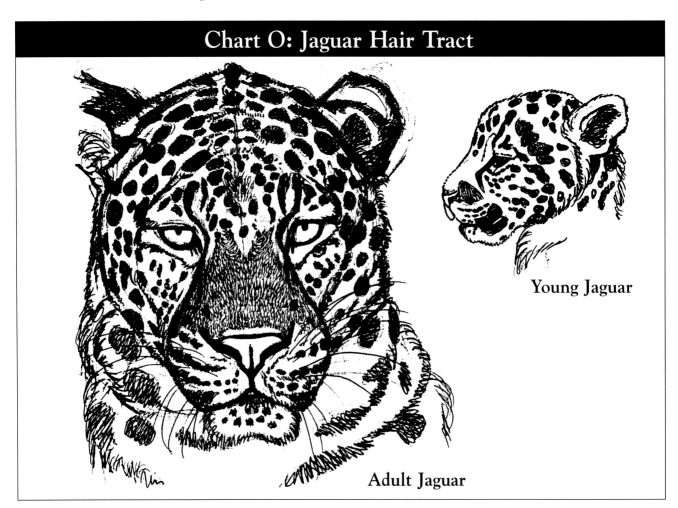

Chart O: Jaguar Hair Tract

Young Jaguar

Adult Jaguar

Carving, Burning and Painting a Lion

On the following pages, you'll find a step-by-step demonstration on how to carve, burn and paint a lion. You'll see how to lay out a pattern, block in the basic shape of the lion, add texture with gouges, burn in details, and apply acrylic paints.

Demonstrations such as this are important to show carvers how to go about completing a project. They are especially helpful to beginning carvers. However, it is important to note that each carver will eventually develop his own style. To that end, following step-by-step procedures can be detrimental to a carver's creativity. I encourage you to use the following demonstration as a guide. Study the techniques and then move on to develop your own carving style. There are many ways to carve, burn and paint. And none of them are wrong!

Artist and author Desiree Hajny paints a lion.

Further Resources

Sculpturing a Red Fox out of Wood Video *by Desiree Hajny*

This 83 minute video focuses on creativity, carving, woodburning and painting. Cost of the video is $30. Available only in North America.

Send orders and inquiries for futher patterns to:
Desiree Hajny
1707 Shiloh, Wichita, KS 67207
(316) 682-5349

Step-by-Step

Carving a Lion

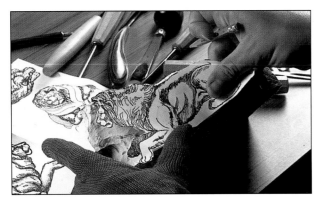

1. With the wood grain running horizontally or vertically, lay the pattern on the wood making sure it matches up with the grain. Cut the basic shape of the lion on a bandsaw.

2. Trace around the pattern with a pencil or felt tip marker. Using a knife, carve down to those lines.

3. Using the top-view pattern, draw in the top view of the lion and carve the body to those lines.

4. Draw in the centerline. This line will represent the backbone.

5. Draw on the leg line and cut along it with a parting tool. This cut will separate the wood of the base from that of the lion.

6. Using an 8mm, #8 gouge, cut to the lines of the side silhouette of the lion's head.

7. Take measurements from the head, front and top views of the pattern and transfer these measurements to the wood. Use the centerline as a point from which to measure.

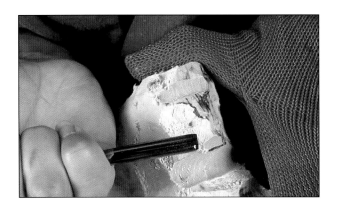

8. Use a 6mm or 8mm, #10 gouge to trim the chin area.

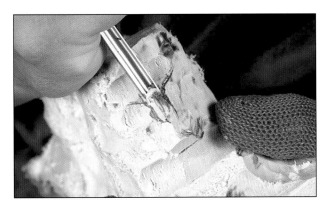

9. Using a 4mm, #8 gouge, shallowly cut out the area above the bridge of the nose and between the eyes.

10. With an 8mm, #8 gouge, cut the temple area back toward the ears just slightly.

11. Refer to the front view pattern and draw in the mouth and nose with a pencil.

12. With a gouge, trim the wood down to these areas of the muzzle.

13. After removing that wood, mark in the muzzle area using the side-view pattern for reference.

14. Carve away the area of the mane in front of the ears so you can return to work on this area later.

15. With a carving knife, make a stop cut under the nose pad and then undercut it. Stop cut the mouth area and undercut it as well.

16. Check over your work utilizing your reference materials.

17. With an 8mm, #10 gouge, cut under the chin area toward the front leg area scooping out the wood between the two front legs.

18. Draw in the front paws. With a parting tool, cut around the front paws to accentuate them.

19. With a pencil, draw in the front and back leg detail and the tail.

20. With a parting tool, define the belly and leg lines.

21. Next, define the tail using a parting tool.

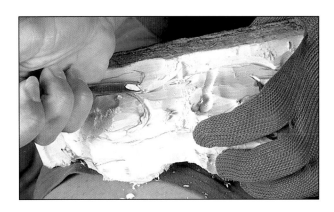

22. Then, use the parting tool to outline the back foot.

23. Define the lumbar region and the inside of the back leg with an 8mm, #11 gouge.

24. Taper the backbone with an 8mm, #10 gouge.

Step-by-Step

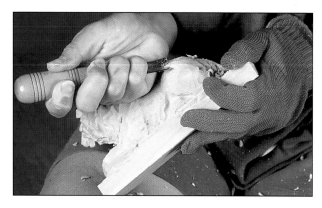

25. Round off the knee and thigh areas with a 12mm, #8 gouge.

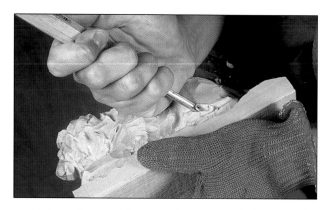

26. Use a 5mm, #11 veiner for a softer definition of the heel tucked under the rear end.

27. Cut and taper under the belly with a 5mm, #11 veiner.

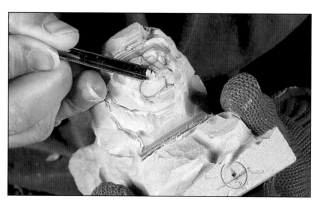

28. Using the same tool, make a v-cut below the nose pad.

29. Use the veiner again to define the area behind the muzzle under the eye socket.

30. Use a 6mm, #11 veiner to sweep the mane toward the center of the chest.

31. Shape up the chin by rounding off the squared corners with a 6mm, #10 gouge.

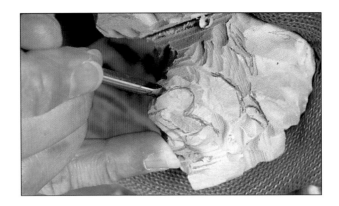

32. Make sure the chin fits neatly under the muzzle.

33. Stop cut between the toes or use a parting tool to define the toes.

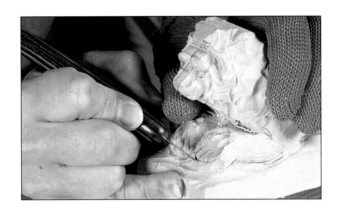

34. Separate the two front feet with an inverted pyramid cut.

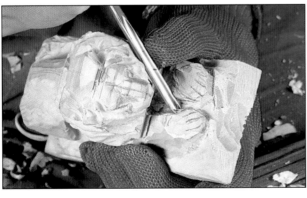

35. Scoop out more wood between the legs with a 6mm, #10 gouge.

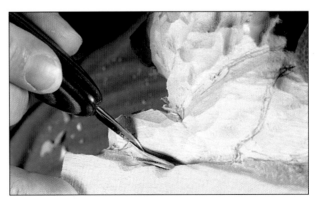

36. Using the pattern as a reference, make stop cuts following the wrist area and then make an inverted pyramid cut.

Step-by-Step

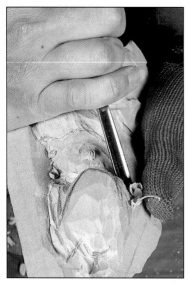

37. Define the stretch of skin between the back leg and lumbar region with a 6mm, #11 veiner.

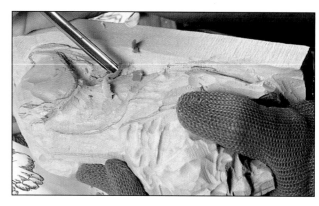

38. Using the top view as reference, v-cut the shape of the back foot.

39. Stop cut the heel area and use an inverted pyramid to accentuate the rear end and heel areas.

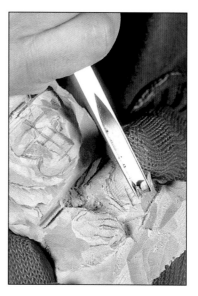

40. V-cut the front feet.

41. Then v-cut between the toes.

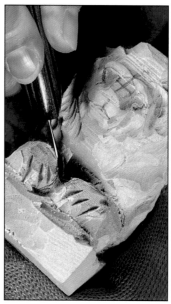

42. Use a knife to make an angled cut above the wrist.

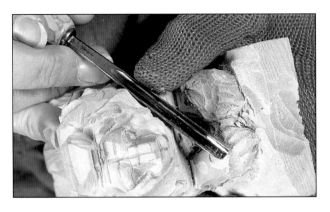

43. Using a 6mm, #10 gouge, sweep the top part of the paws behind the toes to indicate knuckles.

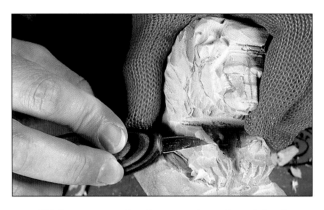

44. With a carving knife, taper the sides of the front paws, rounding off the square sides.

45. Next, taper the inside of the wrists with a carving knife.

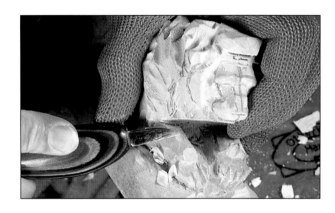

46. Still using the carving knife, round off the upper limb above the wrist.

47. Shape up the area around the tail, rounding it out with a parting tool.

48. Outline the inside of the tail with a parting tool.

49. Still using the parting tool, separate the toes.

50. Use a 5mm, #11 gouge to gouge in the sides of the rib cage where the skin is squeezed together by the back leg and the loose skin on the belly.

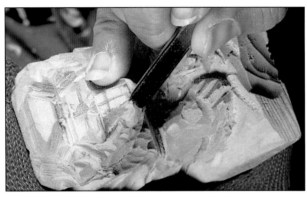

51. Touch up the muzzle and shape around the nose pad and the sides of the bridge of the nose with a 3mm, #11 veiner. Use the parting tool to define the sides of the nose as well.

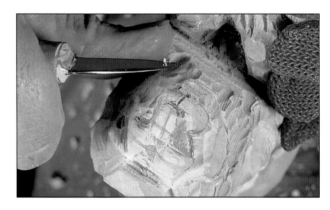

52. With a carving knife, angle the mane toward the center point of the neck area.

53. Round out the bridge of the nose with a knife.

54. With a 6mm, #10 veiner, scoop out the eye socket gently so you don't tear into the bridge of the nose. Using a pencil, draw in the shape of the eye. Check to make sure the eyes are at right angles to the centerline.

55. With an eye punch, push lightly to mark in the eyes. Again, check the line up. When you are satisfied with the position of the eye, apply the eye punch again and push harder.

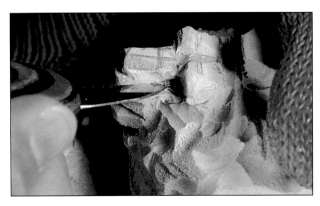

56. Push a detail knife in from three sides, making an inverted pyramid for the tear duct area.

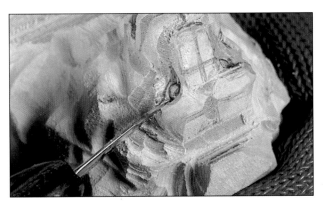

57. With a carving knife, stop cut behind the eyeball, following the brow line. Undercut this line to give the lion peripheral vision. This cut will open up the sides of the socket so the eye can be seen from the side view.

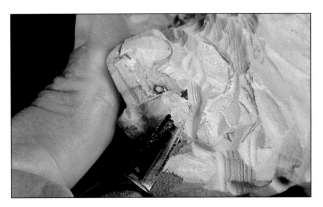

58. Using a detail knife, cut in the temple area. This area sinks in behind the eye and brow and in front of the ear.

59. With a parting tool, separate the mane and shoulder so you can go into more detailing. Soften the lion features with sandpaper or buff the surface area with scotch bright. Cut out any rough areas. Leave the mane and end of the tail rough for heavy texturing.

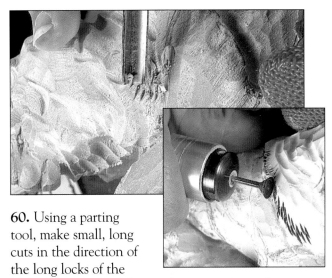

60. Using a parting tool, make small, long cuts in the direction of the long locks of the mane. The inverted diamond cone can be used in much the same way as the parting tool to get the illusion of the mane texture.

2. Outline the eyes with tip 1A or 10A.

1. Using burner tip 1A or 10A, outline the eyeball to give the illusion of dark eyelids. Before burning in the pupil, mark its position with a pencil so you don't end up with a cross-eyed lion.

3. As you burn the pupil and the eyes, keep your hand and the lion braced steadily, so you don't end up with eyes that are marked incorrectly.

4. Check the eyes and make any necessary corrections.

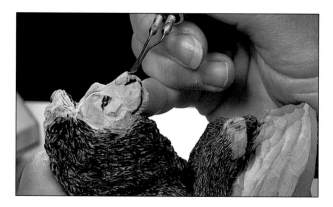

5. Outline the mouth under the muzzle and slowly burn along this line to give the illusion of black lips.

6. Burn in the nostrils and outline the nose pad. Map out the special shape of the nose with a pencil. Use the charts for shape references (Chart H, page 17).

7. Following the hair tract chart (Chart N, page 25), use short strokes to burn in the small hairs on the forehead. Remember to change the direction of the hair as it crosses the centerline.

8. Continue burning with short strokes on the side of the nose. Try not to make the burn marks parallel. You're trying to create the illusion of fur. Cross the marks over each other once in a while.

9. Using burner tip 1A or 10A, burn in the hair around the eye socket. Start around the eye and burn outward in the direction of the hair flow. This will give the illusion of the tiny hairs found there.

10. Burn in the hair on the chin. The strokes below the muzzle hang down. Those on the upper side of the muzzle also hang down from the nose pad. Utilizing gravity, use a stab-pull motion, following the direction of the fur. Don't be tempted to put too much space between the hairs to save time.

11. Use the stab-pull method on the lion's body and face. Keep in mind the subtle change of fur along the backbone. For the long hair on the mane and tail, follow the texture and break it down further by using pulling motions to burn across the high points between cuts.

Step-by-Step

Painting a Lion

1. Using a #00 detailer or pointer, mix dull white acrylic paint with water until the paint reaches a milky consistency. Apply the white around the eyes, muzzle, chin and inside of the ears, pulling in the direction of the burned texture.

2. Apply the white color on the white parts of the body with a large #6 round or #10 flat brush.

3. After marking in the white areas, mix in a tan color made from yellow oxide mixed with raw sienna. Start at the forehead area and nose and brush in the direction of your burn marks.

4. Using the same color combination, brush the color under the chin along the mane.

5. Mix yellow ochre and white with tan and thin the paint with water. Brush the color on the forehead, temple, top of the muzzle and below the eyes. Mix a dark brown into the sunken areas for shadows. The colors will bleed together on areas that are highlighted. Add a touch of white to the already wet areas to enhance them.

6. Paint the backs of the ears, allowing the tan to bleed into the whites of the ears. Paint this color on the iris of the eye also.

Carving Big Cats

7. Mix black and raw sienna to a thin consistency. Brush it on the mane and the tip of the tail. Also, dab it into the middle of each ear, letting it mix with the white.

8. Use a mixture of the yellow ochre, raw sienna and white on the legs, shoulders and body. The tail backbone is brownish. Remember to mix the browns on the shadowed areas and whites on highlighted areas.

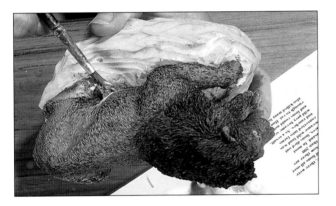

9. Check over your piece and repaint areas that might have been over-mixed. Brush whatever you have left on the palette on the base. Make sure the paint is dry before proceeding with the next step.

10. Using a #9 round or #8 flat stiff-bristled brush, touch the brush tip to the white paint and scrub lightly on the palette. Pull the paint in the opposite direction of the texture.

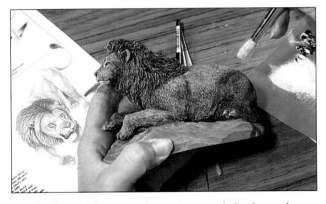

11. Drybrush the rest of the piece and the base also.

12. Using a #00 spotter or detail brush, paint in the tiny details such as the dark brown dots where the whiskers are located.

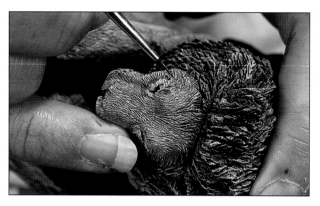

13. Paint in the dark brown behind the eyes by pulling downward.

14. Paint in the details on the muzzle for whiskers.

15. With brown, pull the color behind the cheek and toward the mane.

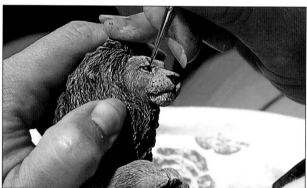

16. Mark in the eyebrow with brown.

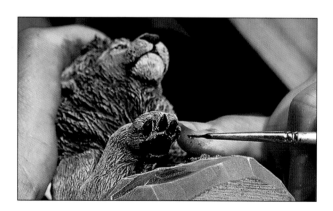

17. Paint in the pads on the bottom of the feet with black paint.

18. Using black paint and the #00 spotter or detailer, pull paint along the woodburned lids around the eyes.

19. Mark in the cheek area with brown.

20. Use a spotter to pull black paint along the eyelids.

21. Dot in the pupil. The paint should sit in the burn area and not run into the iris. If it does, let it dry and repaint the iris with brown and yellow-white.

22. Apply a tiny white dot to the upper part of the iris, remembering where the sun is hitting each eye. You are presenting the illusion of the reflection of the sun.

23. Darken the nose with black. Pull the paint through the cleft under the nose and continue it on the mouth. Remember the black lips.

Using, Altering and Creating Patterns

In this chapter, I have included several patterns—a jaguar, a tiger, a lion and a lioness. The poses of the subjects in these patterns are interchangeable. For example, the tiger can be carved in the jaguar's relaxed position, and the jaguar can be carved in the tiger's walking position.

Advanced carvers can also alter these patterns to create new poses. Simply use the reference photos, skeletal illustrations and muscle drawings in the research section of this book as a starting point. You can get some ideas of other poses from the photos in the front of the book.

To use these patterns "as-is" for a project, duplicate them on a photocopier, enlarging or reducing them as you see fit. Place a piece of carbon paper, carbon side down, between the pattern and the wood, and trace over the lines of the pattern with a pencil or other pointed object. Remove the pattern and the carbon paper from the wood. The lines that you traced over will appear on the block of wood.

Pay close attention to the direction in which the wood grain runs. All of these cat patterns, with the exception of the lion, should be laid out on the wood with the grain running vertically. The lion can be carved with the grain running vertically or horizontally.

I suggest the following dimensions to carve cats from these patterns. You may, of course, reduce or enlarge them as you see fit.

Lion—$6^3/4$" long, $4^1/2$" high, $4^1/4$" wide
Lioness—$8^1/4$" long, $5^1/4$" high, 4" wide
Tiger—7" long, 4" high, $3^1/2$" wide
Jaguar—9" long, 5" high, $4^3/4$" wide

Poses are interchangeable. For example, the tiger can be carved in the jaguar's pose and the jaguar in the tiger's pose.

Enlarge pattern on photocopier to 110%

Enlarge pattern on photocopier to 110%

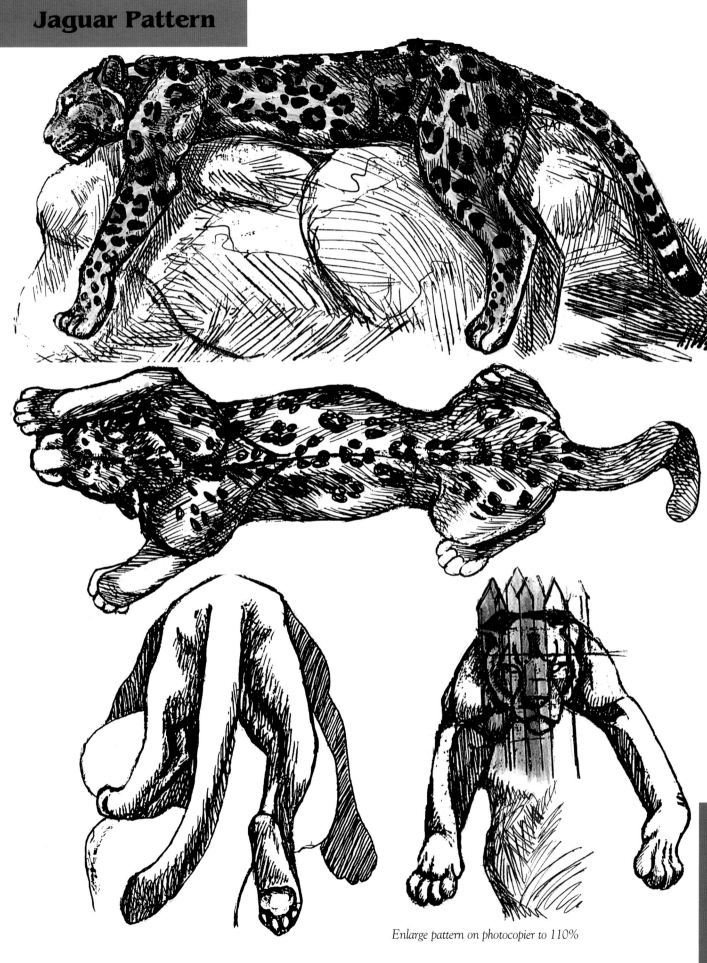

Enlarge pattern on photocopier to 110%

Patterns

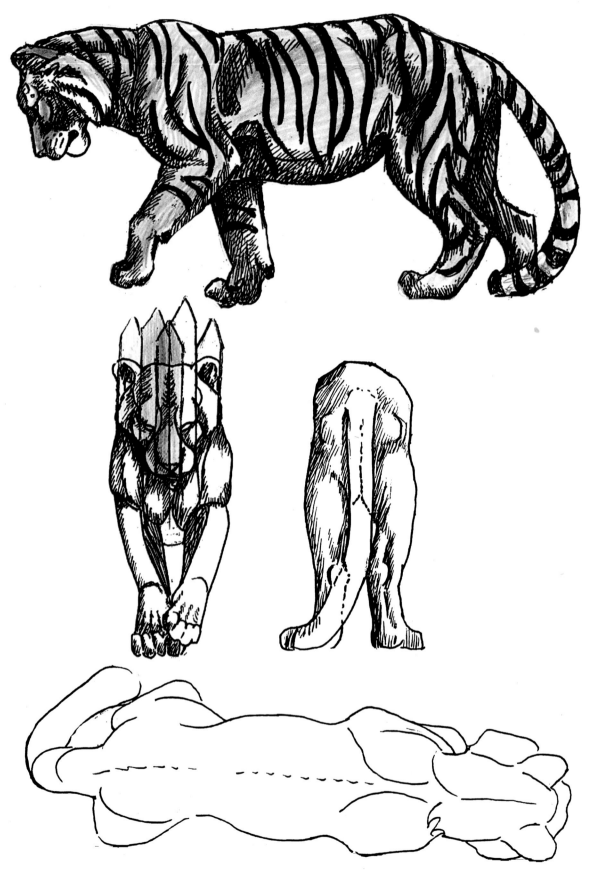

Enlarge pattern on photocopier to 110%

Enlarge pattern on photocopier to 110%

Patterns

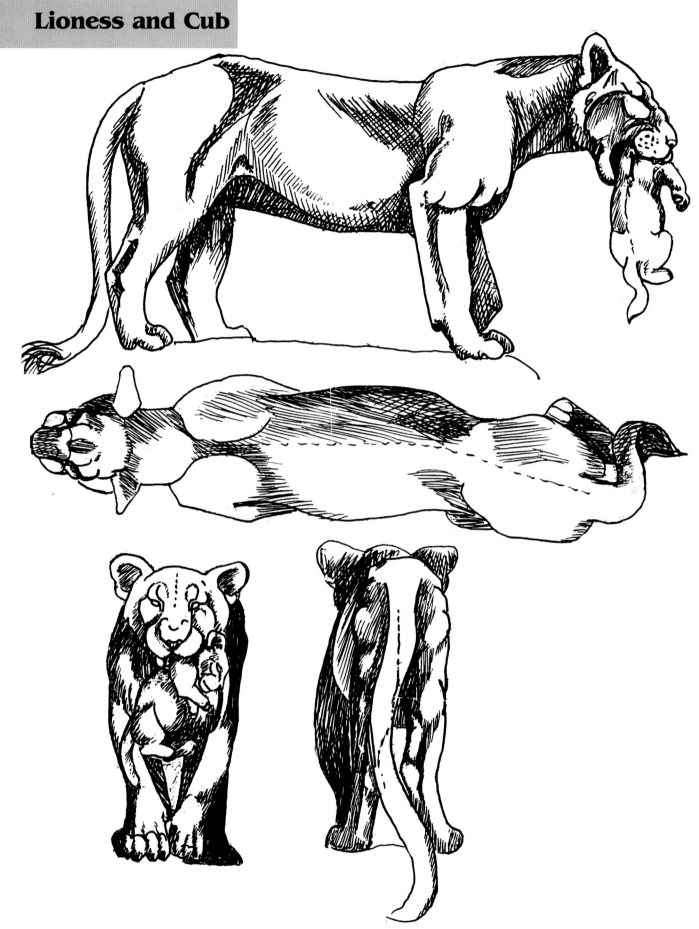

Enlarge pattern on photocopier to 110%

Index

Bones
  legs 10
  while leaping 14
  while walking 12
Charts
  Bone Movement While Walking 12
  Bone Movement While Leaping 14
  Common Woodburning Mistakes 22
  Ears 18
  Eyes 16
  Feet 21
  Jaguar Hair Tract 26
  Leg Bones and Muscles 10
  Legs 20
  Lion and Lioness Hair Tract 25
  Noses and Mouths 17
  Skeleton Illustrations 7
  Skull 8
  Tiger Hair Tract 24
  Woodcarving Cuts 15
Cheetah
  carvings of iv
Cubs
  pattern 49
  pattern with lioness 50
Ears
  carving 18
  woodburning 18
Eyes
  carving 16
  woodburning 16
Feet
  carving 21
  woodburning 21
Hair Tracts
  jaguar face 26
  lion face 25
  lioness face 25
  tiger 24
Jaguar
  bone movement 12, 14
  carvings of 1
  ears, carving/burning 18
  eyes, carving/burning 16
  feet, carving/burning 20
  hair tract 26
  leg bones illustration 10
  leg muscles illustration 10
  legs, carving/burning 20
  mouths, carving/burning 17
  noses, carving/burning 17
  pattern 47
  photos of 10,11
  research information 10–12
  skeleton illustration 7

  skull illustration 8
Legs
  carving 20
  woodburning 20
Leopard, Snow
  carving of iv
Lion
  bone movement 12, 14
  carvings of 2
  ears, carving/burning 18
  eyes, carving/burning 16
  feet, carving/burning 20
  hair tract 26
  leg bones illustration 10
  leg muscles illustration 10
  legs, carving/burning 20
  lion, female (See Lioness)
  mouths, carving/burning 17
  noses, carving/burning 17
  pattern 45
  photos of 5, 12–14
  research information 12–14
  skeleton illustration 7
  skull illustration 8
Lioness
  carvings of 3
  hair tract 26
  pattern 46
  pattern, lioness with cub 50
  research information 10–12
Muscles
  legs 10
  while leaping 14
  while walking 12
Mouths
  carving 17
  woodburning 17
Noses
  carving 17
  woodburning 17
Panther, Black
  carving of 1
Patterns
  altering 44
  cub 49
  jaguar 47
  lion 45
  lioness 46
  lioness with cub 50
  measurements 44
  tiger 48
  transferring 16
Skeleton
  lion 7
  jaguar 7

  tiger 7
Skull
  illustrations of 8
Technique
  carving, general 17–23
  carving, step-by-step 28–37
  ears 18
  eyes 16
  feet 20
  gouge cuts 15
  knife cuts 15
  legs 20
  mouths 17
  noses 17
  texturing, general 23
  woodburning, general 23–25
  woodburning, step-by-step 38–39
  painting, general 25–26
  painting, step-by-step 40–43
Tiger
  bone movement 12, 14
  carvings of 4
  ears, carving/burning 18
  eyes, carving/burning 16
  feet, carving/burning 20
  hair tract 26
  leg bones illustration 10
  leg muscles illustration 10
  legs, carving/burning 20
  mouths, carving/burning 17
  noses, carving/burning 17
  pattern 48
  photos of 6. 8. 9
  research information 5–9
  Siberian (see Tiger, Siberian)
  skeleton illustration 7
  skull illustration 8
Tiger, Siberian
  carvings of 4
  research information 9–10
Woodburning
  common mistakes 22
  ears 18
  eyes 16
  feet 21
  jaguar face 26
  legs 20
  lion face 25
  lioness face 25
  mouths 17
  noses 17
  tiger 24